Unicorn fish

Manta ray

Whale shark

Green sea turtle

Blue-ringed octopus

Blue star

Reef squid

Giant clam & Clownfish

Whitetip reef shark

Royal blue tang

disc

Mantis shrimp

Tube coral

Brain coral

The Coral Kingdom

For William: barely a polyp when this book began, but now so much a part of our reef.
L.K.

For Matt: thank you for always keeping my head above the waves.
J.W.

© 2018 Quarto Publishing plc

First Published in 2018 by words&pictures,
an imprint of The Quarto Group.
6 orchard Road, suite 100
Lake Forest, CA 92630
T: +1 949 380 7510
F: +1 949 380 7575
www.QuartoKnows.com

Consultant: Michael Bright

A CIP record for this book is available from the Library of Congress.

ISBN: 978 1 910277 67 6

9 8 7 6 5 4 3 2 1   17 18 19 20 21
Manufactured in in Dongguan, China, TL122017

The Coral Kingdom

Laura Knowles & Jennie Webber

words & pictures

Come and see the coral reef, beautiful beyond belief.

From up above you'd hardly know so much is going on below.

Coral larvae, young and free, drift on currents through the sea, until they find the perfect spot; a rocky shelf, a sunken yacht.

Together, polyps build a home,
layer by layer, hard as bone.

Where fish and shrimp and sea horse thrive,
sharks patrol and dugongs dive.

Over many thousand years, this colossal reef appears.

Though growing at a snail's pace, it's visible from outer space.

Every creature plays its part,
to make this living work of art.

Let's take a dive! We want to know:
what colors do the corals grow?

Coral crimson, red and rose, where camouflaged small creatures pose as coral branch or feathered arm, staying tucked away from harm.

Coral yellow, bright and bold, a salty sunset flecked with gold.

Where sea stars cling and mantas roam, garden eels defend their home.

Coral turquoise, emerald, jade, living jewels that must not fade.

As turtles cruise among the weed,

upon their backs the cleaners feed.

Coral purple, royal and grand,
a throne emerging from the sand.

As gentle minke whales glide past,

a blue-ringed octopus holds fast.

Coral dark and inky black, where skulking, nighttime hunters track

their prey through crevices and cracks. Silently, a shark attacks!

But coral white's a ghostly fright! Something here is far from right.

The warming seas don't suit the reef. They'll bleach if there is no relief!

To keep this treasure of the sea, we must choose greener energy.

The time is now, the chance is brief!

Stand up and save the coral reef!

What gives coral its color?

Corals get their color from zooxanthellae, algae that take in carbon dioxide, process it through photosynthesis (like all plants), and give off oxygen and nutrients, which the coral polyps use. In this way, coral polyps and zooxanthellae live together as one, and need each other to survive. This is what scientists call a "symbiotic relationship."

What causes coral bleaching?

Climate change is making the oceans warmer and more acidic. These conditions make the zooxanthellae produce toxins, which puts the corals under stress and causes them to get rid of their zooxanthellae. Even small increases in temperature can have a big effect on a coral reef. Without the zooxanthellae, the coral looks pale white, yellow, or brown, which is why the process is known as coral bleaching. If the corals stay bleached for too long, then the coral itself will also die.

Can't the coral just grow back?

Coral reefs grow slowly, so this means that once a large area has bleached and dies, it will take a very long time to grow back. If the oceans stay warm and acidic, then the coral won't regrow at all, and could even go extinct.

Why is the coral reef important?

The coral reef is more than just coral. It is an ecosystem made up of all sorts of marine life that live together and rely on each other for food and shelter. From microscopic plankton to huge sea turtles, there are more different sorts of living thing in a coral ecosystem than nearly any other place on Earth. If the coral reef dies, then many other animals will lose their home and could become endangered or extinct.

So that in future, all will know this coral kingdom down below.

What can we do to help protect the reef?

The coral reef is in danger, but there are changes that everyone can make to help protect it:

Reduce air pollution

Pollution from burning fossil fuels in cars and airplanes causes global warming, raising the temperature of the oceans. Whenever possible, walk, cycle, or take public transportation instead of traveling by car.

Save energy

Factories and power stations also burn fossil fuels. Try to reduce the energy you use at home by turning off lights and electronics, and wearing extra layers instead of turning up the heat. Discuss with the person who pays the electricity bill whether they could get their electricity from a company that uses renewable energy.

Use less water

The less water you use, the less wastewater will pollute the ocean.

Plant a tree

Trees help reverse global warming, by absorbing carbon dioxide in the atmosphere. They also help reduce the amount of water, known as runoff, that flows into the ocean and can contain polluting chemicals.

Garden responsibly

Encourage your parents not to use pesticides and fertilizers in their garden that can harm ocean life.

Don't be a litterbug!

Even if you live far from the sea, litter can reach the ocean, polluting the water and harming ocean life. Plastic will float in the ocean for thousands of years, and it breaks up into small pieces that are eaten by fish, birds, whales, and other sea creatures.

Snorkel responsibly

If you visit a reef, follow guidance on how to do so without causing harm. You can join a cleanup group to help remove trash while you explore the reef.

Spread the message

Let others know how important the reefs are. The more people who know and care about the coral reef, the more will be done to help save them.

Find out more

Coral Reef Alliance: *coral.org*
Great Barrier Reef Foundation: *barrierreef.org*
Kids Against Climate Change: *kidsagainstclimatechange.com*

Trigger fish

Coral hermit crab

Star coral

Sea fan

Dugong

Anemone

Anemone

Crown of thorns

Lipstick tang

Starfish

Brittle star

Sea cucumber

Pygmy seahorse